TWO LANDS

TWO LANDS

Gwenda Schanzle

To our children

Tony Tory Philip Pamela

Order this book online at www.trafford.com
or email orders@trafford.com

Most Trafford titles are also available at major online book retailers.

Printed in the United States of America.

ISBN: 978-1-4269-0261-1 (sc)
ISBN: 978-1-4269-0262-8 (hc)
ISBN: 978-1-4269-0263-5 (e)

Trafford rev. 10/22/2011

 www.trafford.com

North America & international
toll-free: 1 888 232 4444 (USA & Canada)
phone: 250 383 6864 ♦ fax: 812 355 4082

Acknowledgements

Phoenix Zhou – for his elegant cover design.

Miriem Pinczower - without her patience, and editing/ reading skills this anthology would never have seen the light of day.

Barry Lee – for his computer expertise without which this manuscript might not have reached Canada intact.

Ottone Riccio - who taught me and encouraged me to write poetry.

Contents

Two lands to love

Clouds hang low
pattern a deep blue sky

The start of summer
 perfumed gardens soft warm air
a day for dreams the other
garden half a world away
the sky a paler blue
mountains a deeper one
called a mountain day

We walk the woods pick
wild flowers listen for bird
songs winter passed
a garden about to bloom after
the snowdrop and first daffodil
winter leaves late it always
does never by March

In the North Country
where summers seem short
autumn flows miraculous
before a stark November gray
glistening white of fresh snowfall
long winter nights with
a sparkling sky

Past dreams you say
allow me the dreams the house
on the hill the seasons
sugar maples in early spring
when the sap starts to run
fires lit in the sugaring house

New bird songs in this south land
wreathed in yellow sands rolling seas
   and its mystery

War Bride

How strange a thing is fate
when it picks you up on
 a perfect summer day and
takes you to a different place
fate had us in its grip he was walking
down the path tall with eyes as
blue as sky a war torn uniform and ready
to say *May I join you* we smiled and laughed
then fell in love as fate so wished for us

Accents new to the ear
sang through our streets
United States Marines lifted from battle
to recover a soul time clocks click fast
passions soar on wild winds of war
the minute is precious believe we are
made for each other so a day in July
I take his name church bells ring
flower hats young men in green uniforms
the air is clear a raging world forgotten
 in romance of one afternoon

An early dawn from a window
I watch my warrior turn that corner to
waiting
ships swinging at anchor the company of
men

he will take once more into war no tears
the day would come left unsaid
the words that hung in every corner of the
room
when where again again did come
the adventure began to cross an ocean
and one continent slide into a motionless
bay in a sunrise of gold

A mountain love affair

the Rockies painted in pink in afternoon sky
we will have a house in the mountains one day
that is the future the now two nomads
captives by war we live for the day sit curled
on the dunes above the Atlantic setting sun
at our backs we listen to waves
sing on the shore lie in spring grass
greener than a salad bowl
watch the snow geese fly north overhead
through time and the roughest of seas
we made it to shore

To journey that long curving path
so planned by fate

Other Side of the Coin

Farewell to the dunes
the cottage and sand fleas
the deep south *Darlin' yer know*
with every sentence

To Washington
Hey kiddo I gotcha you betcha
breakfast grab a stool
at the corner drug store
fried eggs sunny side up
get it down fast there's a line behind
and not a blue suit in sight
ribbons and stars on uniforms
a Murphy bed that comes down from the wall
heave it up in the morning light
a wall of fluttering sheet
to enliven the dusty paint

Until one day
we are about to be three crisis
fate where are you and fate did come
not a minute too soon
a house a kitchen and two bedrooms
 but babies are laundry fate forgot
panic first morning no dy-dees
they are all soaking in
the one bath tub no basket
or pegs and no clothes line
a ladder down to a basement tub

We're on our own
no baby manual or how-to book
forget the war this is more serious
with a tear in his eye
and down on one knee
Marine cap in hand
he pleads for help from
the Dy-dee Wash man crisis averted

Each morning young Marine major
carrying large soggy bag sits alone
in standing room only commuter bus
    Wartime Washington

Goddess

I remember
when I was young beautiful
wearing the finest
tracery of ornaments
 and jewels people came with bells
and drums admired me
worshiped me
I was arrogant you were old

I heard
your whisperings in the night
did not reply I was the wonderful thing
they came to see you the old jungle life
I was the temple
then a new one was made
and I left behind

I wished
I could die did I sleep all those years
as you crept closer and closer
until your tendrils kissed my lips
wrapped my body
in your sinuous vines

I awoke
to be one with you
the great jungle home
your stillness at noon night filled with life
no longer old walls of stone
I am part of the ageless canopy

Alice In Her Wonderland

Under a plain blue sky
peace and calm

soft air as in a crystal glass
the smallest leaf hangs motionless

nothing moving only thoughts
in a garden of flowers

no ghost of breeze steps
through the leafed plane tree

easy to dream of Alice
as she slips tip toe quiet

into her painted world
she does not fade

in her upside world of words
even if over there somewhere

guns and
bombs still reign

and I still live in peace

The Public Garden

Boston Massachusetts

No shadow cast no sky to see
   In the silent world of falling snow

no breeze to stir the dried out leaves
   I stand as caught in a quilt of white

the moment between the evening and night
   no path to walk in a white iced world

my footprints slowly filling are gone
   as sifting snow paints

my shoulders ever deepening white
   the stone arch bridge
I cross each day
surreal as a floating sculpture is

will I remember The Garden heavy with snow
   in the pale grey light of evening

when flower beds are red with tulips
the pathways filled with hurrying feet

I stand for a moment then turn back
to the world of yellow lights

Crisis Commentary

2008

Where is the wild eyed Tiger
who swung from his Tower
to smash the *Money Wheels*
the ones that spew out affluence
In paper notes

Wild eyed Tiger
you've made a mess
shredded paper
lives in free fall
no landing strip or butterfly net

Forgotten your street
cleaning crew highways now
choked with money dust
Tiger where the hell are you
we need your clear road map

Mariner

Your passion
white sails curved by the wind
taut lines singing your music
you join the ancient mariners
when you put out to sea
and time is left behind
like the band of white ribbon racing
down the starboard beam to spill
into a swirling wake

You are Odysseus
sailing out to meet
the rose colored fingers of dawn
then on to the islands and far beyond
the sea your canvas ever changing in light
until the blue of the sky turns red in the west
you bring her about spill out the wind
to rest for the night the sky your ceiling
embroidered in stars

But remember the days
when the seas turn to rage with
the force of the gale and the drive of the wind
you laugh at the sting of the rain on your face
head straight for the thundering wave to meet
the challenge again and again shouting
and laughing as the helmsmen of old
your element
    the sea and the wind

The Searcher

Seeker what do you find
when you fly with the winds

A world both hard and soft
the silence of deep falling snow
shining lakes woods of white birch
they give their beauty to keep
wild storms great mountains
their strength

The endless
highways that blister
the feet and empty the soul
then give it back
in one starlit night

The ponds
are rich and deep
they give their undergrowth
of intellect that clothes me
I am the dry sponge

Soaks up the songs in old cities
the music of long waterfalls
excitement of buffeting storms
the ponds teach thought
I come back clad

Sea Story

She sits
at the water's edge
curled like a mollusk
each spreading wave
tells of the lover
the fair haired boy
she kissed on
a wind swept cliff

The one who went to sea
seduced by the Cyrenes
to be Neptune's own

She sits and waits
for the song of
the fair haired boy
to beckon her
into the deep
she will lie with no other
than the one
she kissed upon the cliff

A cruel lover is the sea

A Troubled Dawn
Tsunami

In chaos
of moving plates
a giant is born it carries
an ocean upon its back
racing across the sands
until bared by land on
a different shore in fury
sucks in spews out
smashing drowning
all in its path

The sun shone
bright that summer day
a quiet sea the fish will bite
food for the table all is well
with death unseen
only the gulls see the giant
fly to the hills beyond

Under a dark
night sky no star to guide
a torn few on a hill behind
grab at the grass in fear
sleep troubled sleep with
the taunting lap of a
gentle wave they grab at
the grass again

Across the line to the east a ribbon of light
and a rooster crows.

Lover

My lover
        my friend
you would like me
to write love poems
In a perfumed garden
white jasmine
silver strands
of moonbeams
it is not the time
in which I live

I must write what is around me
beyond our garden gate

How much you ask
do I love you it is
the strength of a supple vine
your touch your sigh
your laugh
when we curl up together
and awake
        each day

The Cello

When the old year
slips to the hill behind

The corks have popped
and all have left
the silence calm and sweet

Just you and I
this one last time

No longer can the fingers
slide your strings
release the tones to flow
as cream and fine aged wine

The sparkle of sunbeams
tones polished over the years
that stay in the ear

Bon voyage beloved friend
I must grow old
and you are blessed to sing

Summer

Come outside
the storm has passed our passions calmed
come stand among the grass upon the cliff
feel the wind run fingers through our hair
watch the gulls catch the wind to sail
above the long horizon line

Stay outside
look for small things in the fields
of new mown hay hear the summer
hum of locusts bees and butterflies
find wild orchids sheltered in the woods

Let us take
time into our hands
savor it feel it leave behind
what is has been and may be
love is not picked from the apple tree
we make it fresh each day

No Spring

Enemies
recalled in image
become real

Put on the tight armor of enemy
green horizons leave your world
there is no room for them

No time for dreams
no time for love or spring
the songs are fight and kill

In the hard armor of hate
a hate that must be taught
before you learn to think

Two Worlds

Come back into our garden
bury your face in the roses
feel the silence of still waters and
sleep sound sleep to the rustle of
a breeze through the mulberry leaves
and look not out to the far beyond

I carried my baggage for too many years
cannot forget the fires of war
those who play with toys that kill
guns spreading hate that rages faster
than a wild grass fire seeps in
the baggage left outside the garden gate

Baggage filled with the screams of
a child in the night the tears of a woman
they ring louder than hymns and prayers
the fear of a flash in the midnight sky
the one that destroys not your garden
the one out there beyond our sight

I will stay a time with you
by still waters your world
and ask you to see into mine

War Games

Castles on high
Walls of stone
Rivers of sadness
Rivers of blood

I take my harp upon my back
walk from the fields to the castle on high
Maker of music singer of songs
make us to laugh the Gatekeeper cries

The queen wears her crown her ladies in white
like fragile white roses they sit in a row
I sing with my heart they sing with their lips
and blank are their eyes

Rivers of sadness
Rivers of blood
Castles on high
With walls of stone

The clash in the courtyard of armor and spears
it drowns out the music and smothers the soul
I look up at the walls they are laced with tears
that glitter and shine like shards of cut glass

So I take up my harp I walk to the gate
Maker of music singer of songs
teach us to sing the Gatekeeper cries
I look for the angels that guard the gate

They lay in small pieces I shiver as captive

The Airman

It stands alone part of the land
in a barren field of France

A small brick cairn carefully built
to hold the rough hewn cross
words burnt in the cross-bar read

He came from the sky we buried him here
the year of Our Lord 1916 on these bricks
the moss will grow to shelter him

I see the young face fearless
/in his propeller plane white scarf
flowing in the wind as he spirals down

One fighter that did not return to base
I wept

The B-17
World War 11

White clouds sail
against a deep blue sky

The flight deck quiet
we have dropped our bombs
a tired crew hanging on and letting go
knowing we have a battered plane to
get us home when off the starboard
wing we see a small black fly
       we know what to do

Hold on to your seats we dive
hide and seek but not the game
we look for a lifesaving cloud
then another always the little
black fly in the open sky
ready to make the kill
       parachutes fastened

We sit wonder what the day will bring
across the Lowlands we lumber and dive
to the last cloud in the evening sky
there below the blue of the channel
but above the little black fly
he takes his time to make the turn
       heads straight for the kill

So close to home our luck couldn't last
we wait for the hail of the bullets the dive
to the sea he flies straight in
      Salutes and Climbs

September

A perfect dawn arose
the sun shone bright and
sunbeams danced on water
that Tuesday in September

The day we hear the voice of
horror at the carnage we will see

A carnage born of anger
that sparked the fires of hell

We see it all in black and white
gray wings outstretched fly straight in

Sheets of steel melt into string in
a furnace of flame bodies into dust

We hear a voice from the sky say to
a mother we are all going to die
fighting they crashed in a field
the sky still blue the sun shining

Three Wars

A helicopter rises
over torn rice paddies
shattered forests

Sad to leave Buddy
Nope
Must have been a nice place once
have any family back home
Yup
I guess we won't
have a 'ticker' parade
like my grandpapa
down Fifth Avenue
with crowds it was
Yup a different war

When you joined
the force Flyboy
ever think you'd be flying
a crate like this
No way a ferry route
back to the old U.S. of A.
for them flag covered coffins
Ever wonder
whose bright eyed kid
we have on board
Yup every night
when I can't sleep
Guess it will live
with us as
Vietnam did with my old man
Stupid world isn't it

Yup we wear our wings
and shoulder bars to fly
a hearse across the world

Frustration
USA 2007

Can't you see
beyond your bubble
the damage your guns have wrought

Can't you see
a homemade bomb kills
as well as a rifle or tank

Don't you know
you cannot stride the world
the way you wish

Can't you understand
the power in words
more powerful than your armaments

Can't you listen
and hear the voices shout
their war requiems

Just try sail into the wind
come about and tack close hauled
for a different shore

Where The Wild Flowers Grow

A target
marked in a midnight sky
the bombs hit with a deadly skill
girders bricks mortar smashed
lie in a burning heap
they who slept with dreams now
sleep with the mortar and bricks

The mourners
come to weep and sing their hymns
in a land where once
the grass was green and flowers grew
their songs may never sweep
the flaming candles out
until the guns
have done their work
the twisted heaps are cold

Between
the bricks wild flowers will grow
as requiem for those who lie below

Images

Memory in the mirror behind the eye

Last patch of snow
the first patch of gentian blue
withering winter virgin spring
under the old pine tree

The day you brought Wayward Wind
into the harbor under full sail you
tall in the stern the wind at your back
to bring her finally home

Silence when woods are filled
with snow stark black
shadows from tall white birch transparent
sky in the peace of deep winter

Summer nights in a garden lit by
a thousand stars and a polished moon
moths flutter above we wrapped
In the seclusion of night

The times we walked the beach
a westerly blowing strong
our feet lost in spreading waves
a freighter motionless on the horizon line

Images held in the mirror of the eye

The Quartet

Darting colors woven in sound
violins violas
a river
twisting
turning
threads of gold
cellos like shadows on water
music
that
dazzles
the ear

I – a spinner of words
can never make
translucent tones
fly
to the sky
the scale of an organ
the notes
of the brass

I create black lines
words
words
stamped on a page

You have wings
and take me with you

A World Ahead

Hello Grandson
you joined us this day
the weight of our genes
will lead you where
my new grandson

To challenge the headlands
swept by the winds
fight in wars that
that maim young men
green pastures shadows
and sun and calm seas

Will we together swim with
the fish in their silent world
through supple sea grass
and over the reefs
stroke a marlin and
listen to whales

Shall we watch from a hill
the black night sky
dream of a world beyond
the carpet of stars
a journey into another space
one you may take some day
the one I can only dream about

Your world will I understand
and the sculpture of your soul

Nostalgia

Angels are strange beings
remember the Sunday
we sat in the Shed
heard Mahler
the angels took us to heaven
and let us float back
in time for the final part
that was the afternoon
the swallows swooped
down to join Mahler on
his ramble through the alps
funny the places you go
the experiences you have
on a summer afternoon
at Tanglewood
the angels you meet who
take you on a heavenly trip
even if you have never met

The things one can write
sitting in the sun
with a foot in two lands

Acorn

Great oak
when did you break
from the acorn put down
your first small root

We sit in your shade wait for
the west wind to sing through
your boughs watch the song birds
play in your leaves

We tell you our secrets
our failures our joy
first days of school
loves lost
sons leaving for war

Gales lash around you
tear at your leaves
you give with the wind
your roots holding fast

Old friend
our icon of strength

The Rose

Time
       slipping sliding
punch in punch out
too early too late
       the rod held over your head

Spread it out look at it and
       it flows on dream
the day away under a spreading tree
       the two black arms upon
the round lit face tick on tick on

But remember the moment when
       time stood still
the moment when he gives the rose
       nothing moves
the world turns gold
       the music plays on
the curtain comes down
       and we are moved
but time unmoved sweeps on

Australian Lullaby

Child
   of the drought
will you ever hear the magic
of rain drumming on the roof
spend a day watching raindrops
race down your window pane
run bare foot in soft green grass
will you only know the crunch
of a sun dried land

Child
   of the land
will you know these plains
the way your forebears did
grazing stock and
miles of waving grain to
an endless far horizon
when they held to the gate
waited for the heat of the sky
to soften to gray
the music of rain falling
through leaves tired plains greening

Will you feel the melancholy
and the beauty of this strange land
and all its many parts

Brief Moment

Late afternoon sun
when hills are painted in pink

They suddenly are there
out from their forest
a black mother bear and her cub

That moment in time
two mothers stand motionless
aware of each other and curious

Blue pool water part of our world
between us she stands up tall
looks long then they are gone

Leaving we the trespassers
on her forest land and I
like an immigrant mother who has not

The language to communicate

Elegy

The face
that haunts in the night

She stands in the rubble
left by the tanks and guns
bare legs, black dress worn thin
too tired to cry or greet the dawn
each day and too weary to mend
her splintered world
the child whose eyes are black
with fear and knows no play

Is the wind
that blows the ashes of her neighbors
the same soft wind that blows upon my back
and fills my sails each day

Morning Walk

You ask me about a God
I have no answer to give my God
is not among myths and books

Come stand upon the river bank
feel the beauty of a morning
trees wrapped in mist

The dragonfly skims the surface
of still water parrots chatter flecks
of red and green among the leaves

Let us walk the path to the hill
look on all sides suede colored
paddocks patterned with grazing stock

Valleys mountains the seas
the tiniest fish the greatest elephant
and *Us*

What made it all happen is God
my God

Tasmania 2002

Precious little island
I will come and live with you
stripped clean my baggage left behind
cross the river climb a rounded hillside
to build a garden of lilacs and roses
white lisianthas and lavender hedges

A southern star will fill my night time sky
peace to sleep and dream in crystal air
and awake to the warbling song of
magpies strutting the lawn

Oh precious island
can I remain detached
and strangely without challenge
or will my little mice seek out
the seeds among the baggage
left upon the river bank

And bring them to my door

Far Winds

They sit wrapped in anticipation
fishing for sweet thoughts
(we were a loving family)

Smile as he picks up
the single sheet clears his throat
My Dear Family
When you read this Will
I will be sailing an uncharted sea
with a wind at my back
(they sigh how like him)
For you left to sail a charted sea
I wish only the best
(they straighten and smile)
I leave to you a treasure
more precious than riches
my yacht Far Wind and
her own foundation to care
for her every need cherish her
and she will reward you
every nautical mile you sail

He puts down the sheet
(a patient nod please continue)
that is it the Will is complete
shock waves air turns to ice
they shuffle out

From the back row
a twelve year old boy is shining
his life is made

Among The Bracken

We walked
through the bracken and up to the ridge
the white mist below lay quiet on the fields
looked out beyond the the spring on the hills
this our beginnings with crash of the brass
and the tones of the flute together we sing
  Look up at the magic
    not down at the mist

Summer of life we climb not the ridge
but up to the peaks through maples
and oaks to the great pines above
on to the top look far on all sides
and up through the clouds together
we toast that day on the ridge
  Look for the magic
    not down at the mist

Our garden of flowers rests in full bloom
trees in full leaf make patterns on grass
paths well swept a garden complete
we laugh at the world dance in the street
learned how to love and to laugh and we
sing
  Look up at the magic
    not down at the mist

Sand Castles

Like two nautilus shells
we sit curled by a turquoise sea

I grew up on this beach
built my first sand castle right there

Did you lose your virginity on this beach
the whispered *yes* unlocks a truck of
memories

Winters and summers like no other
racing down sand dunes skiing the heights

Laughter streaming behind no turmoil
we fell so easily into each other

Young flesh sensual in a world
of snow and sparkling waters

We thought it was forever
  We had to grow up

Three Small Poems
Maine – Australia – New Hampshire

Restless ocean
swirling gulls
sail close hauled for shore
your beacon one
lone fir tree wrapped in mist
on the rock bound coast

Ragged hills
sweeping plains silent desert

the soul of a land I do not know
your mystery the whisperings
ancient tales in the moment
of the Dreaming

A brush stroke of light
across the peaks
the pageant of sunrise
like sparkling water flowing
down the mountain side
the magic of new day

Psalm For A New Year

Based on a seven syllable stele

Healing
Laughter
Love
Forgive

Can we heal our only earth

Let the nightingales sing
And lions roar

And heal a world
Of a hate that kills

Spread laughter not anger
For what might have passed
Love send abroad
On wings of the wind

And take the greatest blessing of all Forgive

Love Song

Let me
be all things to you
the supple branch at your side
let me awake you at the dawn
so we together experience
the start of each new day
the marvel of it all

Let us
love each other
and show it to the world
let us be each other's food and wine
dance with Bacchus across
the cracks and rocks storms
and sunlit lands

Let me
cry with you and
learn your songs
and I may sing you mine
let me laugh with you
my gray flannel suit and knotted tie
your bare feet and flower strewn skirt
or the clouds of Zeus hide your sun

Let us
stay as we are until
the dice falls the path fades

Fences

I walked your streets a long time ago
wondered who lived in the houses
no fences no gates green lawns
shade trees and flowers but
the doors were closed to me

Who is inside bleak and cold
do not touch we are precious and old
we see the beyond through shaded
shades safe behind our closed front door

Or children dogs and laughter
Come in but it was not painted
across the open front lawn
so I walked on

Out to the fields slid through
their post and rail fence
breathed the fresh air of escape
and waited with time for the moment

To hear Come in
what took you so long
we have been waiting for you

I had to weave new threads into my cloak

Twin Elms

They were here when I came
    towering above
    a rooftop
Two green kissing bears
    with rounded backs
their snouts just touching

We ate each morning our
    porridge together
filled the imagination
    each evening
with the hurdy gurdy man and
    his dancing bears
in some far distant city square

Now bare space rooftops
    and a ragged aerial
It took one morning with a raging saw
    my kissing bears were gone

What It Is Like

If you find these words
on a dusty page
I want you to know
that I was here

I live the adventure
the black holes slashing storms
then sunshine and calm
flaming colors in autumn
first snowdrop after the snow
the glitter of midnight sky
do you now sail the stars
        as we sail the seas

We climb the high mountain
look far beyond
drive the great plains
write our books our poems and songs
walk the deep forest and
careless of all
        we are given

The dark shadow our armaments
of war that fill the ponds with ashes
a gyroscope will steady
we sleep for a time
in the womb of
       a midsummer dream

The journey will pass
like a wisp of cloud in a racing sky
If you find this page I leave
the love I may
       forget to give

House Cleaning

I wonder
what it will be like
the last day on earth
will I walk my morning walk
that strange unusual day

Will I have time
to say farewell
to my favorite tree
the one I planted
the spring I turned twelve
the years will they
spill out for all to
see or will someone
find them
keep in some safe place

They never
felt heavy to me
some fell out
of a pocket once
I wonder who has them now

Are they still
roaming that city street
my odds and ends
like sailing charts
books and pens

Am I just house cleaning
on a blue summer day

The Smell Of Rosemary

I loved you
the day we met and you for me

We were to be each other's fate
two flying clouds in the wild rush of spring
the tangled growth of a summer garden
hail and rain and winter storm

We take the one same path
through every valley and hill
A journey edged in Rosemary

The Lake

I still feel the excitement
the dark opening in the woods
the long narrow driveway

Leading to summers recalled
and summers now in the brown
shingle house by the lake

I walk the long verandah stand silent
behind the white canoe birch our sentinels
lean against a rounded post

See myself the child racing down the dock
peering through crystal water for a fish
listen to the haunting cry of a loon

The horizon outlined by Mt. Chocorua dark blue
against an afternoon sky a new generation
race down the dock look and listen

The big room the gray stone fireplace
that has heard our stories over and over
from the faded books still the shelves
behind glass doors

The swinging seat under the old pine tree
writing love poems on white birch bark
dreaming the day away on the lake

Time unchanged in the weathered
shingle house it is we who change
feel tired old or become the brash young

The lake brings us back to who we were

Reflection

Six generations have lived
    In the brown shingle house by the lake
      nothing has changed
    the white verandah posts still need paint

The lake no change like satin in the sun
    cousin Madeleine just back from Rome
      she has changed

Dammit she's a cousin
    we didn't think of that five years ago
      what a golden summer it was

No canoe is moored at the dock
    the house will never forget the day
      the lake turned to rage
        and took both Jake and Dirk

The family will never forget
    the night I ruined their sacred game
      drifted off to think of cousin Madeleine
      and trumped my partner's ace

The Years

What do I like most
to slip between white sheets
and find you there our giggle
love or just pillow talk
    silly and intimate

Mornings
our coffee in the sun
the rustle as you fumble with
the paper sigh bang down
your mug then up and out
saying as you always have
here I come to greet whatever
    slam the door

Day's end
the quiet time we sit by
open doors watch an evening
fade from gold to velvet black
wine reflects red on the glass
slowly sip you lean forward
to see a rising moon between
the trees cock your head to listen
    for the last bird call

The small things
among the turns and twists
in the road behind the odds
and ends that stay
the years the kids I argue
you smile my horseplay
your jokes all part of the path
we walk together

First Born

I had a son today
part of me for so many months
 now in my arms
perfect to the smallest eyelash

Our son our stranger
we do not know you yet
it seemed so simple
when you and I were one
 now you are you

We can furnish you with love
but will that be all you want

Shall we journey far together or will we part
we did not think of this in our hour of
ecstasy

Our trip has just begun
Good luck little one

The Deer

Through
a silent forest
the logging trail
soft after
winter snow
carries the memory
of spring
long ago
creaking wagon wheels
axes and oxen
take out great oaks
to carry the sails
for fast clipper ships
that raced the oceans
to worlds far east

We walk quietly
without hurry
 stop
listen to
a first bird call
think the oaks
may green this week
a flash of sunlight
slants through
the pines and beech
three deer
calmly
sharing the morning
in their own space and we in ours

Part of a forest primeval

Soliloquy
to John

An empty chair
behind me on the lawn
I see you there with book in hand
white shorts your body tanned
I hear your voice and feel your touch
but know you are not there

Dear Warrior martini man
I cannot mourn
we had those years what
God or Goddess gave this to us
we took the gift and lived the day
what more
    is there to wish

The Master

Did you try the journey once
fly to close to the sun

Now you sit in your garden
with peonies lilies and books
furnish our minds with words
they flow in rolling
circles sweeping curves

At times thick as wool
or fine spun silk shining

Clothed in your words
we face the highest mountain
walk the soft valleys of Changri la
the hard streets of Manhattan
we love and live

You stay in a garden
safe just to be…

A Choice

Am I the empty face
to show to the world
my dreams stowed
In a helmet of brass
safe and unhurt
      or
Shall I walk through
the open door
climb the steeple
my soul to soar
up through the clouds

Free from the Bible's sin
to live with the challenge

Fractured Dreams

I have not roamed since I was boy
looked with dreams to the hills beyond
all the places a boy can wander
and wonder the stars at night
wild flowers and trees
they came put a gun in my hand
I ran from their guns
to nowhere to nowhere alone

No baggage a dream now fractured
 like the rays of the dawn
through patterns of wire the wire
of a fence that holds me within
a place with no soul
a place without songs
I yearn for the wings of a lark
to soar from the place of nowhere

The boy I once was forgotten
fenced in somewhere
how long how long before they find
a bitter man with a twisted soul
a soul once sweet as a piece of fresh fruit
 now dry and hard with anger
And no clear dawn to bring new dreams

The Shell

You gave me a shell
perfect and fragile
carried by a gentle tide
to a golden beach

I hold it in my hand
feel its ridges
the sands of an ocean floor
the rhythm of waves
in mother-of-pearl

A simple shell
pulls back in time
to sand summer winds
a child's joy
splashing feet
in spreading waves
seagulls sailing under
white cotton clouds

Quiet skies
free from the toys that
shoot to kill

Flash Of Sunlight
Afghanistan 2008

The wind sliced through him
like shavings of ice
no sun shines down
to warm a ceaseless wind

In his hand
a flock of yellow petals
the letter reads
remember the day
we sat in a field pulled
the daisies *love me love me not*

He watched
the petals scatter
and fly like flecks
of gold against the gray
the flash of a summer day
    he threw back his head

Laughed then shouted
    to the hills around
      there is a place where
    the daisies grow

And he heard the ageless voices sing

The Tapestry

Long ago when the world
was very young
a Unicorn looked out to sea
and fell in love with a green haired
Maid dressed in silver scales

Chaste and green haired maiden
touch me with your hand
The wolves are braying at my heels
I dare not turn on them then

Put your hand upon my horn
And come and ride with me
To swim among the stars
At night and live upon a rainbow
On neither land nor sea
We shall weave ourselves in flowers
With threads of green and gold
Immortal will our union be
Of Maid and Unicorn

A Dreamtime

The beach is cold
the cliff behind dark forbidding
gentle waves spread white lace
upon the shore we stand as one
wait for a dawn to bring fresh dreams

A school of fish ruffle the waters
a flock of birds rise from the point
I pick up a cowrie shell feel its
rounded back roll it in my fingers
think cowries are rare upon this beach
we find rare things among the sands
things for the spirit to keep

I look up at the cottage that shelters us
in times of passion in times of calm
I see the gulls soar and sail the moon
cast gold dust across the bay
and through our window frame

His soul is in the cottage on the cliff
and on the beach below

A Matter Of Desperation

Crazy carpenter bee
   I did not recognize you
     the small black knob
    upon the floor
to be caste into the paper bin

I picked you up
   dropped you back
     startled by your
    wlld pulsating heart

Were you in love
   took a wrong turn
    to follow
   some unknown path

I laid you on
   a paper square and took
    you back outside
  were you thinking…
How stupid for a bee to fall in love

Not Much Day

No scudding clouds
sky not quite gray
yet not quite blue
leaves hang still
cliff grasses curled
quiet as though they sleep
sea and sky merge as one
edged in white along
the sands where seagulls
stand contemplate
a day content with itself

I look back to the windswept house
anchored to the ridge
its eyes cast to the sea
the ghosts are still there
the old piano once held our hearts
alone unplayed
the blue willow plates chipped a little
as am I the smell of lavender
and table manners
grandmothers and aunts

The ghosts of a not much day

Mirage

Do not look back
my blue eyed boy
memories are the mirage
a sheet of quivering shadows
in the sands behind
the broken mosaic of years
lost somewhere

Was it worth
those moments of ecstasy
then the slide to nowhere
is the end of a trip
so bleak you clamor for
another flight to oblivion
then the agony
the agony that never leaves

You were in flight to the glitter
of shooting stars before
you were able to walk our hands
had not the strength to hold
your hand bring you back
to some safe place
blue eyed boy
choose a fixed planet
Not a black mirage

The Shield

I carry the invisible shield
the Wayfarer said
polished
to shine with the moon
and play with the sun
shelter the soul from
piercing arrows of Fate
free to journey where
through forests and over the plains

Into your scented garden
of perfect calm
I must sail with the winds
feel the heat of war and
understand its ways
the shouting songs of anger
futility of it all that bypasses
the one clear word
    Compassion

Spring Snow

I felt the silence
the little noises of the night were gone
rustle and scratch of a field mouse
wheels of a truck half a mile away

Sounds smothered
by soft white flakes that hang
in depth against the dark
snow falling in quietness unlike
the drumming of rain upon a roof

I stand at the window
hard to believe
 the white sculptured world where
yesterday's garden a pattern of
paths fields fences

And I was dreaming
of bluebells and tulips
daffodils the sweet smell of spring
this day the doors are sealed I have no
escape
my freedom tethered by a storm in the night

Tomorrow spring sun
Buttercups

Scaling The Heights

If I fly with eagles
sing the wolves
climb the rock face
I sing and I soar and I dare

I have jumped from the rut
and can never go back

If I fill with rose petals
a bower for my love
and dance with the moon
to the pipes and the lute
the shell is then broken
the walls have come down

You will never go back
when you jump from the rut

From Susan

Your voice
an echo through a silent house
your laughter flown with you
we traveled so far together
climbed mountains crossed rivers
walked cities never tiring of
the things we saw

Your last journey
you took alone left me to grieve
I hugged you close called out
your name you did not heed
the cry you had slipped
beyond my reach

Your pear tree will blossom in spring
and I shall drink tea outside at four
see your footprints in the grass…

A Mountain Dawn

Mountain range
  at midnight

Mountains and sky as one
  dark on dark
no stars no moon in
the darkest curtain before the dawn
T
then one fine line of light
  across the peaks
    spills down a mountain side

      Hills flushed
       with gold

    Sunrise the wonder of new day

Words - Words

The molded bench
on which she sits is hard
ungiving as ungiving as
the room in which she sits
a courtroom three lawyers
sit infront she sees their backs
the judge above

Summer sun slants in but brings
no warmth into this unforgiving room
words toss back and forth
like buzzing flies that find no patch
on which to land - words thrown callously

Will she sleep tonight with dreams
and greet a golden dawn or
life torn apart by the force of a pen
    the word Divorce

Commencement

The child
the one who hears
a different drum
untamed
by cap and gown
leading a winding line
of fluttering blackbirds
all poised to fly
and you
my blackbird
ready for
the journey whatever comes

The little one
who said
as she climbed into
her first school bus
Don't worry Mummy
I'll be alright
but was I
my last born on
her first solo flight
into the outside world

The one
I wished could stay
ten years
two months and half a day
untarnished
like a small sail boat
in a following sea
she couldn't
and I couldn't hold her there

One part of motherhood passed
a new one begun

Haley's Comet

We watch
the midnight sky
for one lone traveler
above the red gum trees
a gilded coin with
a curving tail
bright as brass
against a black night sky

Bewitched we watch
we watch
as serene it sails
through crystal air
to a far horizon and beyond

An endless journey
No earth dust in its path

Bird Song

Oblivious of
the shining dawn she's
wrapped in a past
the white clapboard house
a village green chestnut trees
full leafed morning swallows
in the barn the song of the thrush

Another sunrise
back then white cockies cackle
from a distant tree she's
holding to the iron gate
lean leafed eucalypts stud
the paddock spread
sheep searching the edges

No rain again a biting sun
the ever blue sky merciless
before the cool of night
the great silver moon
lighting an old white gum
she loves and hates this land

Wonders will she ever stitch a path
seamlessly...

Starlight

Shepherd Boy
    soul mate in the dark of night

You sail
    a sequined sky and
pass my solitary window pane

What do you wish for
    Shepherd Boy
sing of love to the Weaver Girl

The girl
    with the silver hair and gilded loom
you meet upon the river bank

Did you
    together weave with love
threads of moonbeams into stars

Lovers
    on a separate path
to cross but once a year

Oh Weaver Girl
    and Shepherd Boy
It is a cold universe you travel
    In a glittering starlit sky

The Bushfire

Bleak sterile the silence
woods and towns hills and lives
touched by the serpent's
flaming tongue blazing across
the countryside consuming all
it rides on the wind
    and fed by the sun

Gave no mercy
    those black hot days

They who felt the serpent's
tongue will rebuild again
as mankind does driven by
a stirring in their soul
the whisper of new life green shoots
around the leafless
    gray memorials

And life goes on
    but never forgets

Ride The Wheels

Ride out at the dawn
    ride out on the wheels

Two wheels are all
you need
      optimism in front
spin behind

Take the high way
    to the peaks
to ivory palaces
    and jeweled streets
clear sailing
    no boulders or pits
on the way

Soar speed
    and glide
you are on the right track
    if you ride on the wheels

Optimism to guide
    spin to stay
ahead of the game

Time-Line

The sun slants through
the open half of the old barn door
clean stalls hay strewn feed buckets full
I love the order in a barn tack
carefully cleaned hung upon a peg
listen to the snuffling of the ponies
as if they say *it was a good day*
the excitement of galloping hooves

A crow calls from a tree on the hill
hard unsettling as a baby's cry
and a quiet summer haze hangs
in the air like fine silk gauze
I cross the paddocks feel
a slowing step my body tired
is this the warning the strength
to ride the course must end one day

I think of the three great hunters
that have trusted me and
Seamus O'Sullivan the cocky
Irish pony who never faulted
if the challenge was his equal
what gift to be given the gift of a passion
and ride it to the finish line

Wasteful

Where are they
the fleeting images let go
a band of bright ribbon
flashed across the eye and
gone in the breeze of time
those unrecorded words
Like a throw away toy

A western sky ablaze with a setting sun
two people curled in a swinging seat
what did we talk about so long
it does not matter now
it is the band of bright ribbon
flashed across the eye
the memory that stays and not
A throw away toy

Threads of pain recalled
are the band of gray ribbon
The damaged toy that stays

Au Revoir

Do not knit for me a soft wool fence
tattoo explore across my breast

I want to swing to the far high wire
catch the rings swing to a planet
then somersault back

Feel the mud slide under my feet
race the winds arms stretched out
dance with strangers on rooftops

Challenge the danger laugh at it
who knows what is over that hill
or down a side street

I may be back one day
I will never stop loving

Lost In Mist

I could not tell from the face
that last spring day did he know
where he had left his soul

The years the days the months
hidden away too deep to find
time forgotten forever

Had he lost all memories
our pillow talk the boisterous days
we sailed the bay with kids onboard

We sat with arms entwined
together but apart he looked not
to the sky or out to daffodils

The handsome face the deep blue eyes
a mask to cover a mind out in the mist
he was not to be reached

Not even by me
no romantic ending Sweet Prince
to so long a line of memories

Parting

Dawn came early
filling the house with
light scrubbed clean
a gentle breeze rustles
through the aspens
outside our bedroom door
dew covers the grass like fine silk

We pull ourselves from the bed
smile a half smile
the day must be faced
one takes the shower
one makes coffee
we sit at the little red table
wrapped in time and each other

No tears
the day would come we knew
we stand in the doorway
so close naked yet clothed
the words in our eyes
together when
two words that hang
in every corner of the house

Cross Word Clues

Misery
Lost your mobile
   sore big toe
alone on New Year's Eve

Solution
Take a cruise to somewhere
   ship mates all looking
for lovers tough world

Sanguine
Old men rolling dice
   ex-lover might call
can't remember what
   he looks like
does it matter

Au revoir
lovers parting
   but not forever

Wishful Thinking

Real Christmas is
bare trees of winter
all wrapped in lights
like sculptures they glitter
in clear crystal air
Bell ringers sing on the Hill
a Creche on the Common
with camels and sheep
the magic of Christmas in
        a Christmas card world

Balderdash wistful old age it is
remember
the freezing cold air
that numbs the face
kid's soggy snowsuits
and frozen wool mittens
that dangle from tapes
one to a sleeve
the cloddy snow boots and
knitted wool caps that
        always get lost

When you sit in your garden
all perfumed with flowers
hang the stockings on a warm
        summer's eve

Think of
the snow gear steaming
in front of the fire
under the stockings
so carefully hung
in the hope that the sleigh
with St Nicholas might just
have enough antifreeze
for a blistering cold
          Christmas Eve

Wisdom

You ask about wisdom
   Walk a different street each day
the old sage says
   Collect every pebble
     Feel the eons of age
       Listen to the wind
   And cimb the high mountain
Wisdom is putting it all together

Appendix

When I read the works of other poets, I often wonder what it was that motivated
the writer to choose a particular subject. Thus I am adding this short appendix.

War Bride
This is not one of my favorite works, but every line is true.
We met by happen chance, and the rest is history.

The Other Side of the Coin
May not pass as true poetry - but every word is true without exaggeration,
even to the soggy bag.

The B-17
 A true story told by a friend who, at the time, was a young USAF Captain, flying in the nose of this B-17 as navigator/bombardier – and written in response to the challenge to write a story poem.
.

September
I was still living in Boston at the time of 9/11 and drinking a cup of coffee while watching the 9am news when the program suddenly switched and caught the second plane as it crashed into the Tower. It was like seeing an old black and white movie.

Two Worlds
A reflection of how I felt when I first returned to live in the serenity of distance in my original homeland.

Elegy 2002
A front page photograph in The Boston Globe of a Palestinian woman standing amid rubble left by a night attack on her refugee camp.- somehow it horrified me, as I live in relative calm – how unfair.

Far Winds
I have never been to a reading of a Will. But, this work was fun to write and it still makes me smile.

Mirage
This is sheer imagination.

Scaling the Heights
Written in response to a challenge to write a poem about a rut.

Afghanistan
Also written in response to write a poem about petals.

Three Wars
I happened one evening to see a short clip on the TV of a warehouse lined with flag covered coffins. It hit a nerve and I had to write about it.

War Games
I set out to write a medieval poem with lutes, love, and brocade, but somehow it took off on a different direction.

Ride the Wheels
Written to entertain a morning group, writers included, the subject was Optimism and Spin.

Wishful Thinking
Also written to amuse a Christmas lunch audience in Melbourne, Australia.

Nostalgia
Tanglewood is the summer home of the Boston Symphony Orchestra and the Tanglewood Music Center - situated in the western part of Massachusetts. It is sheer magic.

The Choice and The Shield
These two strange little works were written to accompany an exhibition of metal sculptures.

Fractured Dreams
Refers to the asylum seekers who flee their war torn country. The stories of these people in detention touched a nerve when I first arrived back in Australiia. Thus I had to write this poem.

Gwenda Schanzle was born in Melbourne, Australia. But calls Boston, Massachusetts, her home-city, as she married a Bostonian and lived there, with their children, for more than three-quarters of her life. She started her writing career at 17 when she was asked to write occasional articles for the Melbourne Herald Saturday Supplement on a young girl's view of life around her. She continued as a freelance writer when the time permitted, and commenced writing poetry seriously some years ago. She says "I have always written poetry because I love it but kept those early pieces hidden away in a closet."